Dear Parents and Educators,

Welcome to Penguin Young Readers! As parents and educators, you know that each child develops at his or her own pace—in terms of speech, critical thinking, and, of course, reading. Penguin Young Readers recognizes this fact. As a result, each Penguin Young Readers book is assigned a traditional easy-to-read level (1–4) as well as a Guided Reading Level (A–Q). Both of these systems will help you choose the right book for your child. Please refer to the back of each book for specific leveling information. Penguin Young Readers features esteemed authors and illustrators, stories about favorite characters, fascinating nonfiction, and more!

Tick-Tock!: Measuring Time

LEVEL 4

GUIDED
READING
LEVEL **Q**

This book is perfect for a **Fluent Reader** who:
- can read the text quickly with minimal effort;
- has good comprehension skills;
- can self-correct (can recognize when something doesn't sound right); and
- can read aloud smoothly and with expression.

Here are some **activities** you can do during and after reading this book:
- Create a Timeline: This is a nonfiction book about time and how it is measured. When you read nonfiction, you often find many dates in the text. Using the dates and facts in the book, create a timeline to show the history of telling time around the world.
- Comprehension: After reading this book, answer the following questions:
  - How many hours are in a day?
  - What is the difference between an analog clock and a digital clock?
  - How many days are there in a week?
  - About how many weeks are there in a month?
  - How many months are there in a year?
  - How often do leap years occur?
  - How long is a decade? A century? A millennium?

Remember, sharing the love of reading with a child is the best gift you can give!

—Sarah Fabiny, Editorial Director
   Penguin Young Readers program

*Penguin Young Readers are leveled by independent reviewers applying the standards developed by Irene Fountas and Gay Su Pinnell in *Matching Books to Readers: Using Leveled Books in Guided Reading*, Heinemann, 1999.

To my entire family, thanks for
all the good times!—GS

PENGUIN YOUNG READERS
An Imprint of Penguin Random House LLC

Smithsonian
This trademark is owned by the Smithsonian Institution and is registered
in the U.S. Patent and Trademark Office.

Smithsonian Enterprises:
Christopher Liedel, President
Carol LeBlanc, Senior Vice President, Education and Consumer Products
Brigid Ferraro, Vice President, Education and Consumer Products
Ellen Nanney, Licensing Manager
Kealy Gordon, Product Development Manager

Smithsonian National Museum of American History, Kenneth E. Behring Center:
Carlene E. Stephens, Curator, Work and Industry Division

Photo credits: Flickr: page 4 (Ron Cogswell). **Library of Congress:** pages 16, 18, 29 (top), 34, 35.
National Archives: page 29 (bottom). **Smithsonian National Air and Space Museum/Symmetricom,
Incorporated:** page 30 (bottom). **Thinkstock:** cover (front) (Dimedrol68/iStock),
(background) (RYGERSZEM), (front flap) (choness/iStock); page 3 (siur/iStock);
page 6 (seanfboggs/iStock), pages 7, 12 (monkeybusinessimages/iStock); page 8 (mapichai/iStock);
page 9 (top) (tawatchaiprakobkit/iStock), (bottom) (hstiver/iStock); page 10 (AndrewScherbackov/
iStock); page 11 (Tpopova/iStock); page 13 (tatyana_tomsickova/iStock); page 15 (top)
(Creatas/Creatas Images), (bottom) (olm26250/iStock); page 17 (Lai leng Yiap/Hemera);
page 19 (ttsz/iStock); page 25 (choness/iStock); page 26 (ttatty/iStock); page 28 (Katrina Brown/
Hemera); page 30 (top left) (A_Pobedimskiy/iStock), (top right) (VvoeVale/iStock);
page 40 (jurisam/iStock). **Wikimedia Commons:** page 21 (Olaf Tausch); page 22 (Jakub Halun);
page 24 (Marine 69-71); page 27 (Walters Art Museum); page 31 (dronepicr); pages 32–33
(NationalAtlas.gov); page 36 (top) (David Iliff), (bottom) (Alvesgaspar); page 37 (top)
(Chris 73), (bottom) (Pablo Costa Tirado); page 38 (top) (ajari), (bottom) (King Eliot).

Library of Congress Cataloging-in-Publication Data is available.

ISBN 9780515159035 (pbk)   10 9 8 7 6 5 4 3 2 1
ISBN 9780515159042 (hc)   10 9 8 7 6 5 4 3 2 1

PENGUIN YOUNG READERS

LEVEL
FLUENT
READER
4

Smithsonian
TICK-ToCK!
MEASURING TIME

by Gina Shaw

Penguin Young Readers
An Imprint of Penguin Random House

Contents

What Is Time?

How many times have you asked these questions: When is bedtime? What time do I have to get up? When is school over? What time is dinner?

But have you ever asked what *is* time?

Time is the measured period of when things happen or exist.

People keep track of time for many reasons. It helps them plan their days or meet goals. It reminds them when things happened in the past or what may happen in the future. To tell time, people use clocks, watches, and calendars.

Any Minute Now

A clock or watch is used to keep track of the seconds, minutes, and hours in a day. Clocks and watches use a steady beat or movement to track the change in time.

Say "One-Mississippi" out loud. That was one second. There are 60 of these seconds in a minute. There are 60 minutes in an hour, and 24 hours in a day. That's how long it takes the earth to rotate on its **axis**, an imaginary line through the middle of the earth, around which the earth spins.

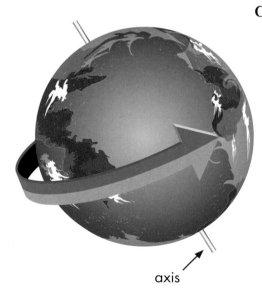

axis

It is daytime when the part of the earth where you live faces the sun. Night comes when the part of the earth where you live faces away from the sun.

Analog and Digital

Most people use an **analog** or a **digital** clock or watch to tell time.

This is an analog clock. The numbers from 1 to 12 go around the edge of the **clock face**.

The hour hand tells what hour it is.

The second hand tells how many seconds have passed since the last minute.

The minute hand tells how many minutes have passed since the hour.

The first set of numbers tells the hour.

The second set of numbers tells the minutes.

This is a digital clock. It has two sets of numbers. You read them from left to right. If you're checking the time on your cell phone, it will probably look like this, too.

A.M. or P.M.?

There are 24 hours in a day. But a clock or watch usually has only 12 numbers on it. So, people use a.m. and p.m. to be clear about whether they are talking about day or night.

When you catch the school bus at 8:00 in the morning, that's a.m. But when you go to bed at 8:00 at night, that's p.m. Any time before noon, or **midday** (12:00), is a.m. and any time after noon, is p.m.

Mark Your Calendar

Calendars measure time, too.

There are 7 days in a week: Sunday, Monday, Tuesday, Wednesday, Thursday, Friday, and Saturday.

There are about 4 weeks in a month and either 30 or 31 days in a month. (February is different. It usually has 28 days.)

There are 12 months in a year: January, February, March, April, May, June, July, August, September, October, November, and December.

One year is made up of 52 weeks.
There are also 365 days in a year, except
when it's a **leap year**. That happens every
four years. In a leap year, an extra day
is added in February.

With a calendar, you can tell what month, day, and year it is.

Here's a fun way to remember how many days are in each month.

"Thirty days have September,
April, June, and November;
February alone has twenty-eight.
All the rest have thirty-one
except in Leap Year, that's the time
when February's days are twenty-nine."

There are ways to measure a long time, too.

A decade is 10 years.

A century is 10 decades or 100 years.

A millennium is 10 centuries or 1,000 years.

Back in the Day

Long ago, people woke up in the morning when it was light. They went to bed when it was dark. They only knew two times: daytime and nighttime.

Eventually, they began to understand that the sun appeared to rise and set each day and that the seasons—fall, winter, spring, and summer—happened in the same order over and over. Some people noticed that as the seasons changed, so did the position of the sun in the sky. This was the beginning of telling time and keeping track of it.

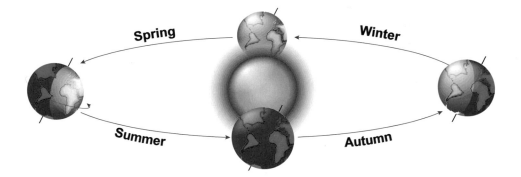

Tools for Telling Time

Thousands of years ago, people created tools to help them tell time.

In ancient Egypt, people built tall stone monuments called **obelisks**. The obelisks cast shadows on the ground. The direction of the shadows told people what part of the day it was. These timekeepers did not work at night or if it was a cloudy day.

Obelisk

Egyptians, Romans, Greeks, and the Chinese used water clocks. These timekeepers measured the flow of water into or out of a container that had markings on its sides. The markings told how much time had passed based on the amount of water that dripped through. Water clocks *did* work in the dark or when it wasn't sunny.

A Chinese water clock

Egyptians built a better device to keep track of time: the sundial. It still used the sun and shadows. It also divided time into chunks called "hours." Egyptians knew that the length of the sundial's shadow varied at different times of the day.

You can still find sundials in people's gardens or in public places.

The largest sundial in the United States is in Carefree, Arizona.

An hourglass is also called a sandglass clock because it uses sand.

Hourglasses were also used in the ancient world. Sand poured from the upper glass bulb to the lower one through a tiny hole. This took one hour. Then the hourglass was turned upside down to start again.

Clock faces were introduced in Italy in the 1300s. They only had one hand, the hour hand. Roman numerals were placed around the face: I, II, III, IV, V, VI, VII, VIII, IX, X, XI, XII. At that time, most people did not know about Arabic numbers: 1, 2, 3, 4, 5, 6, 7, 8, 9, 10, 11, 12.

Clocks like this were very large. They were usually built in towers in cities and towns.

This clock tower in Venice, Italy, was built in 1496–1497.

A mechanical watch from 1530

The **mechanical** watch was first made in France, Germany, and Italy around the same time in the early 1500s. It was small enough to be worn on a belt or around the neck. But this watch only measured hours.

In the 1600s, the first **pendulum** clocks were built. A pendulum is a weight that moves steadily from side to side. It can help a clock tick regularly. Pendulum clocks kept better time than any clock that had come before.

A cuckoo clock's pendulum

The first wristwatch was invented in the late 1800s. It was meant to be worn by women as jewelry. At the time, men carried pocket watches. They wouldn't wear wristwatches.

A pocket watch in an ad at the movies, around 1912

Women at war also wore wristwatches.

During World War I, soldiers who were busy fighting or flying couldn't stop to pull out their pocket watches. So, men started wearing wristwatches, too.

Quartz clocks were made in the 1920s. Inside this clock, a battery sends an electric current into a quartz crystal. This makes the quartz shake or **vibrate.** This movement is part of what moves the clock's hands. Quartz clocks were more accurate than pendulum clocks.

Quartz

Insides of a quartz wristwatch

Atomic clocks tell the time to a billionth of a second. They were first used in the 1940s and keep the most exact time of any clock.

An atomic clock from the 1990s

Smartwatches were invented in the twenty-first century. They can be used to tell time, make calls, text, send e-mail, get directions, read news or books, listen to music, or play games.

An Apple smartwatch

Time Zones

By 1880, more and more people around the world were using clocks and wearing watches. But because the earth rotates, it was day and night at different times in different places. This caused problems when people communicated or made plans. Time needed to be **standardized,** or accepted as a rule, throughout the world.

In 1884, most countries agreed to divide the world map into 24 time zones. All clocks within

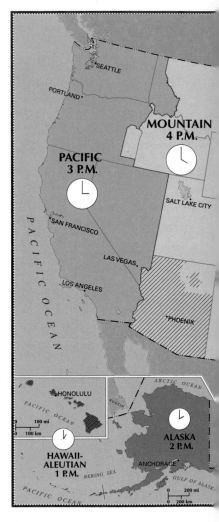

each time zone kept the same time. Each time zone was one hour ahead or behind the time zones on either side of it. (The measurement started at Zone Zero in Greenwich, England.)

The time zones of the United States

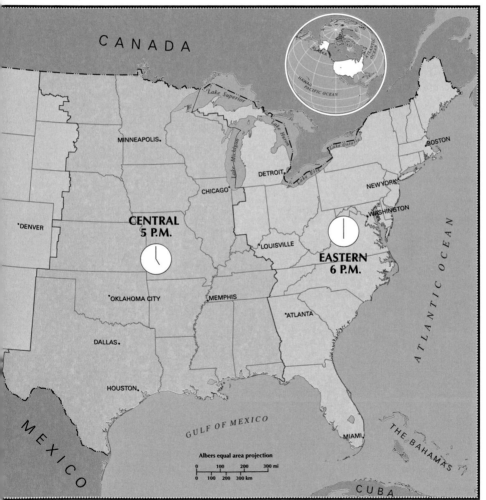

Saving Time

In 1915, Daylight Saving Time (DST)
came into use in some countries.
Daylight Saving Time is also called
"Summer Time" in many places around
the world. "Spring forward, fall back"
tells people to set the clock forward one
hour in the spring at the beginning of
DST and to set it back one hour in the
fall when DST ends. People benefit from

Daylight Saving Time. In the spring and summer months, they have more sunlight for outdoor fun and play. On fall or winter mornings, they don't have to drive or walk to school and work in the dark.

Daylight Saving Time helps people save energy, too. They don't have to use lamps, heaters, and air conditioners as much as they would have if they didn't turn their clocks forward or backward. DST started in the United States in 1918. However, two states, Hawaii and most of Arizona, do not use it.

Famous Faces

Here are some famous clocks from around the world.

This Strasbourg Astronomical Clock was built in France in 1843. It has a mechanical rooster that crows every day at 12:30 p.m.

The Elizabeth Tower in London, England, is better known as Big Ben. That is the name of the tower's giant bell that rings out the hours.

The Rathaus
Glockenspiel
in Munich,
Germany, has 43
bells and 32 full-
size mechanical
figures that act
out scenes from
German history.

This clock in New York City was
completed in 1913 in honor of the
opening of the Grand Central Terminal
train station.

Cosmo Clock 21 is a digital clock
built into a giant Ferris wheel in an
amusement park in Yokohama, Japan.

The Makkah Royal
Clock Tower Hotel
in Mecca, Saudi
Arabia, has the
largest clock faces in
the world. They are
lit by a million lights
at night.

It's About Time

When you need to make time, remember . . .

60 seconds = **1 minute**

60 minutes = **1 hour**

24 hours = **1 day**

7 days = **1 week**

4 weeks = **about 1 month**

52 weeks = **1 year**

12 months = **1 year**

10 years = **1 decade**

100 years = **1 century**

10 centuries = **1 millennium**

Glossary

analog: a clock or watch with hour and minute and sometimes second hands

axis: an imaginary line through the middle of an object, around which the object spins

clock face: the part of a clock or watch that shows the time

digital: showing the time with numbers and a colon instead of with hour and minute hands

leap year: a year of 366 days instead of 365, with February having 29 days instead of 28. A leap year happens every four years.

mechanical: working by machinery

midday: noon or 12 o'clock in the middle of the day

obelisk: a four-sided monument that narrows at the top, and ends in a pyramid

pendulum: a weight that moves from side to side at a regular rate

quartz: a mineral

standardized: used or accepted as a rule

vibrate: to shake back and forth